Modern
Private
Gardens

Modern Private Gardens

SUSAN and

GEOFFREY JELLICOE

Abelard - Schuman

London New York Toronto

London Abelard-Schuman Limited 8 King Street WC2

New York Abelard-Schuman Limited 6 West 57 Street

Toronto Abelard-Schuman Canada Limited 896 Queen Street West

CONTENTS

INTRODUCTION

There are over forty gardens in this book, all planned by landscape architects or other professional designers. The gardens are private and comparatively small, and have been chosen from examples coming from many parts of the world. They have been arranged irrespective of country and lead from the enclosed to the open space. Although they are visually very different one from another, there is a certain consistency throughout that gives food for thought; the fact that they are all contemporary is an insufficient explanation. Why would a garden by Sir Edwin Lutyens, for instance, be out of place in this assembly of gardens? The quality of design of a Lutyens garden is as good as anything shown; and the fact that a Lutyens-Gertrude Jekyll garden requires much maintenance, an overriding factor in the modern world, does not account for the sense of discord. It is rather that the *spiritual need* for gardens has changed in its requirements. To understand this more fully, and to draw conclusions, we can turn for enlightenment to two sources, history and contemporary painting.

Until recently, gardens throughout the world were geographically separated into the two hemispheres of east and west. The civilisations and philosophies of the two cultures were totally dissimilar. Very broadly, it may be said that the urge of the west towards the creation of gardens arose through fear of environment, whereas that of the east had its origins in precisely the opposite. The appreciation of this difference is of immense importance in the modern world, as the two cultures begin to amalgamate.

The western garden began in Mesopotamia. It was an artificial oasis, not only physically in a land of desert but culturally in the world of ideas. It developed into the Persian paradise garden, which embodied the concept of heaven brought to earth, and was a place of philosophical repose in a hostile world. It was well-watered, geometrical and peaceful, with protected flowers and plants; it was cut off from the barren environment by high walls. The idea of the enclosed paradise garden runs through all Moslem architecture, and later through mediaeval architecture (especially in the monastic cloister), until the coming of the Renaissance in Italy. Then it was that the garden triumphant marched out into its environment, an architectural extension of the house. Nature was being conquered by man, and trim hedges and pollarded trees everywhere showed a mastery of material which echoed the parallel human conquests of lands and peoples outside Europe.

The outlook upon nature in the eastern hemisphere was very different. It was an attitude of reverence, which reached its zenith as a religion in the Zen Buddhist gardens of Japan in the early sixteenth century. In historic Japan, man was not the centre

Introduction

of the universe; he was a comparatively modest part of a cosmos too vast for him to understand. The Japanese, cut off from the diverging intellectual developments and explorations of the west, were compressed within their island by a single overwhelming neighbour, China, from whom they had acquired their culture. Unlike the inhabitants of the Middle East, they loved their island scenery, which was friendly in climate, geography and wild life, and comparatively free from foreign invasion. All the visible world of rocks and plants and humans was in alliance against the two common and invisible enemies, earthquakes and tornadoes; the house and garden together were a symbol of this concord. In form, the Japanese garden was an abstract miniature of the island scenery, a whole world contained within a small space. The house was always modest, built of timber, and transitory; in contrast to that of the western world, which was monumental and designed for earthly immortality.

The island scenery of England has many elements in common with that of Japan, but culturally it has been fertilised by the storm centre of the Mediterranean. As England began to rise to world power in the seventeenth and eighteenth centuries, the instincts that belonged to her own environment surged up and ejected the foreign virus, which had expressed itself most forcefully in the formal avenues that covered the countryside. The romantic rolling country, the groups of trees, grass and water that gave rise to a new and gracious pictorial art no longer seemed hostile to man; the Englishman, like the Japanese, now loved his scenery. But it was not his religion. This extrovert ideal landscape was closely related to his aspirations to world conquest, for the extension of space (mainly through the ha-ha or sunken fence) was limitless; William Kent "leapt the fence and found all nature was a garden", the owner's garden.

English botanists following in the wake of commercial expansion brought back a host of new plants from all parts of the world. These innovations were seized upon with enthusiasm by the general public, who crammed their gardens and greenhouses with the latest discoveries. The only opponent of this new wave was William Robinson, whose theories on the use of native plants are of profound interest to present-day landscape architects; his influence can, indeed, be seen in several of the gardens shown here.

As the superficial understanding of horticulture increased, the sense of form deteriorated. At the beginning of this century, when new art forms were breaking upon the world on the continent, Sir Edwin Lutyens, for all his original genius, was turning back for inspiration to the restricted days of the Renaissance to find the philosophy as well as the physical proportions of his basic form.

All the gardens illustrated in this book stem from the next, more fundamental revolution in men's minds, which first made itself apparent through the artists. If a date could be fixed, it would be 1907, the date of the completion of Picasso's "Les Demoiselles d'Avignon". Simultaneously, Einstein had conceived a theory of space which was to alter western man's whole attitude to hitherto accepted laws and to his own personal relationship to the universe. Instead of being the centre of this universe, man was, at least physically, a very modest fragment. Instead of having finite boundaries, space was limitless and infinite, whether upward and outward, or downward and inward. Whereas time and space had always been conceived as separate dimensions, it was now becoming clear that they were interlocked to form a four-dimensional continuum. Time can distort space as we know it, just as space can distort time. All the absolutes upon which western civilisation had been based were struck aside, like the struts of a ship about to be launched. Most important of all for the future of garden design, the ordinary man had emerged as a thinking machine and a personality in his own right. To continue the analogy of the ship, man began to reconstruct a personal environment around himself to provide the security and reassurance of a cabin. We must now examine the requirements of this cabin, and translate them into those of a garden.

In the small and physically confined space of modern gardens, man is now absorbed in creating whole worlds in which the imagination can adventure. Perhaps above all he is seeking to escape from the world of bricks and mortar into a primitive, disordered world of his own. The two elements in the process of designing this world are *form* and *content*.

Form, or shape, is by far the most important ingredient of any garden. It is the ingredient most likely to be overlooked by the layman, who may otherwise equal the professional landscape architect in originality of ideas and (in England especially) in the choice and arrangement of plants. Form is the disposition of space; unlike the content, whose availability in principle remains constant throughout the ages, it is peculiarly susceptible to changes in personal needs and to mental attitudes. Physically, the gardens of the modern world are innumerable and small, and must essentially be private. For the most part, they cannot extend visually beyond their boundaries, because congestion is too great. However, the shape within the available space is no longer tied to the rules of garden design formulated at different periods of history. The reader can judge of the variety that is possible, simply by seeing the examples that follow. This variety stems primarily from the character of the owner, and secondarily from the inventiveness and ability of the landscape architect to translate the owner's needs into reality.

What is more difficult to comprehend, and even to be consciously aware of, is the sense of abstract design that links them

all together. If we visit a gallery of modern painting anywhere in the world—London, Tokyo, New York or Rio de Janeiro—we find that behind the visual and literary associations belonging to that particular part of the world, there lies an abstract art that is universal in its appeal. So it is with gardens. Just as the mind is responding, in abstract art, to shapes which it appears to seek and even to crave, so it responds to shapes in landscapes; these too may evolve in endless variety, only limited by adaptation to practical needs. Like a painter, the designer of a garden may be unable to explain how he has groped his way to the result; he is working within the subconscious, and his appeal is to the subconscious. Two gardens that illustrate the modern break-up of form and the consequent change from the space design of history are numbers 3 and 5. They are complementary to one another.

It is easier to recognise and comprehend the part played by the *content* of a garden, for this is visible to the eye and can be analysed. As in the furnishing of a house, there must be a local flavour, responding to the categorical needs of the owner as well as to the local conditions. A garden is constantly changing throughout the year, so a decision must be made as to whether it is to look well in all seasons, or only in some. In a modern world, a garden must be easy to maintain; for this reason, and because of their smallness, it might be assumed that modern gardens could not compete in interest with the great gardens of history. This is not true, for the smaller the garden, the greater the perception of detail; modern painters such as Graham Sutherland have found, with the scientists (and indeed with the Japanese of the sixteenth century), that the possible depths of discovery into the workings of nature are limitless. Perhaps the clearest example of this infinity is shown in Plate 7B. Another consideration is the philosophical, as opposed to the scientific, exploration and interpretation of nature; this is well seen in the contrasting placing of natural rock shown in Plates 13B and 17B.

And this our life, exempt from public haunt,
Finds tongues in trees, books in the running brooks,
Sermons in stones, and good in everything.

William Shakespeare, *As You Like It*, (II, i)

A business man living in a hotel-less area 3,200 feet above sea-level has made a rooftop guest house and winter garden for his visitors. Life in the guest house is lived among the plants, which are sub-tropical in contrast with the high altitude.

1A Grasses and dried flower heads—not quite flowers—are particularly suited to the paved area that is not quite an open space (covered but not enclosed).

1B Looking out on to the roof garden.

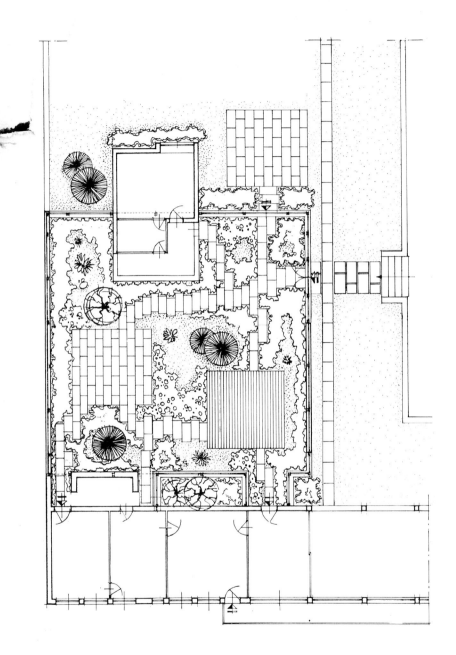

1C The fine tracery outside contrasts
with the heavy foliage inside.

13

2 **WEXHAM SPRINGS,** Buckinghamshire, England | Sylvia Crowe

A scheme for a town garden was carried out in a small court between two buildings at the Cement & Concrete Association's research station. This garden has since been demolished to make way for extensions to buildings.

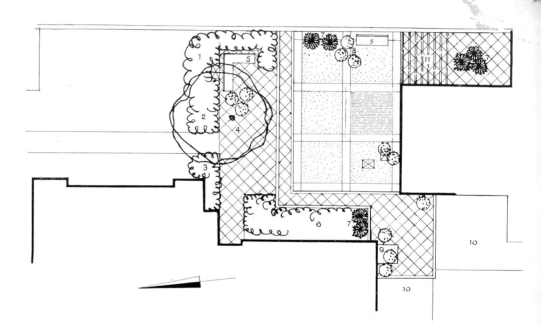

2A Paving is the most suitable floor covering for a small town garden. Here, the space design is dominated by six squares; five of them are cobbled, while the sixth is occupied by a mirror pool. A fountain sculpture in precast concrete units, by Anthony Holloway, rises from the pool to give vertical interest.

KEY TO PLAN
1. Rosa hugonis and Rosa Fruhlingsgold
2. Genista hispanica and Iris cordovan
3. Senecio greyii and Iris cordovan
4. Ex. Almond
5. Seat
6. Viburnum mariesii, Rosa hugonis and Helianthemum wisley primrose
7. Cupressus
8. Flower containers
9. Flower containers
10. Extension of paved area
11. Pergola

2B The floor pattern.

2C There are flower-beds round the sides of the paving, but the main planting is in cylindrical flower containers which are simply standard concrete pipes.

3 **BLACKHEATH,** London, England │ Ivor Cunningham

The garden of a small house at Fox Dales, Blackheath, a recent development by "Span", who have set new high standards in architectural and landscape design for suburban housing. Architects: Eric Lyons and Partners.

3A An architectural setting for outdoor living.

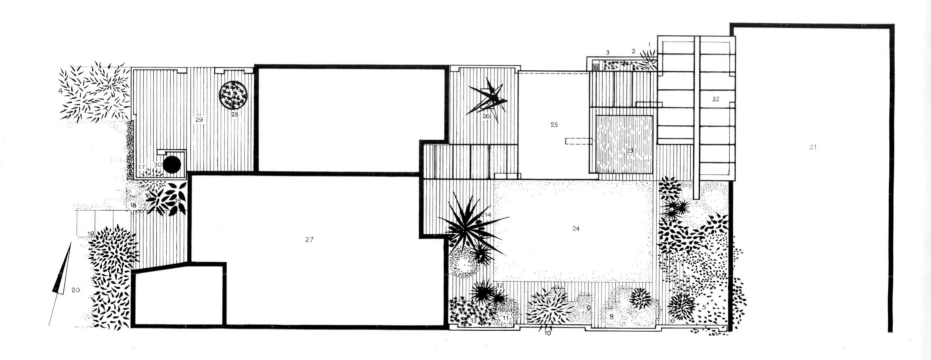

KEY TO PLAN

1. Arundinaria anceps
2. Nandina domestica
3. Podocarpus salignus
4. Prunus laurocerasus zabelliana
5. Nothofagus cliffortioides and
   Carex morrowii variegata
6. Rhododendron hyperythrum
7. Olearia macrodonta major
   and Olearia ilicifolia

8. Cryptomeria japonica elegans
9. Ilex crenata convexa
10. Stranvaesia davidiana
11. Thuya orientalis decusata
12. Sisyrinchium striatum
13. Euphorbia wulfenii
14. Phormium tenax and
    Bergenia crassifolia
15. Rhododendron sino grande

16. Rhododendron arizelum
17. Ilex serrata
18. Picea abies nidiformis
19. Stuartia monodelpha
20. Leucothoe catesbaei
21. Garages
22. Conservatory
23. Pool
24. Lawn

25. Terrace shelter
26. Sculpture
27. House
28. Plant container
29. Courtyard
30. Bin

18

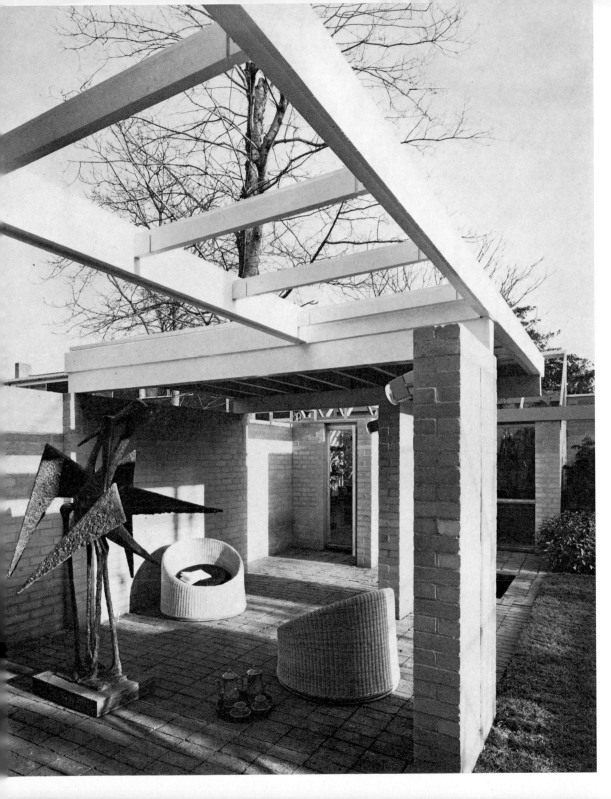

3B There is no finality in the boundaries of this small area. The endeavour has been to create mystery and extension of space through the imagination.

4 **LYNGBY,** Denmark | Andreas Bruun

A front garden with a three-dimensional parterre. Blocks of privet (*Ligustrum vulgare atrovirens*) are clipped into cubes and rectangles of varying heights. The geometrically-shaped beds contain flowers such as asters and erigerons, chosen for their compact growth and because they carry the flower at the top of the stalk; there is also ivy, vinca and *Hypericum calycinum.* Linked to the paved terrace is a small sunbathing lawn.

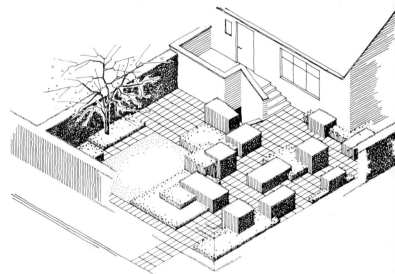

5 **TUNBRIDGE WELLS,** England | A. du G. Pasley

The house stands in the grounds of a larger property and was converted from a coach house and stable block. The main rooms look out over the old stable yard. Lush planting offsets the hardness of walls and the glare of paving.

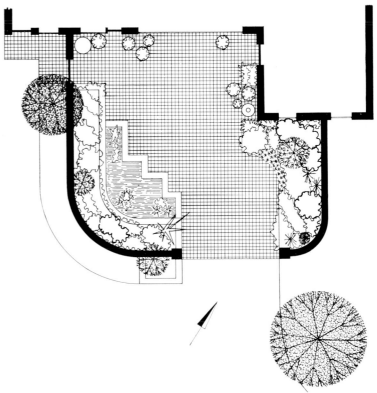

5A Compare with Plate 3B. Here the extension of space through the imagination is made by means of complex foliage in a comparatively simple architectural setting.

5C The huge blue-green leaves of *Hosta sieboldiana* are reflected in a small pool. Against walls colour-washed grey-blue, the shady bed between pool and high wall contains large-leafed evergreens—*Magnolia grandiflora, Rhododendron sinogrande, Fatsia japonica* and *Mahonia japonica bealii*—which will be encouraged to grow up into tree-like forms to throw shadows on the pale walls.

5B The eye is free to wander beyond the garden towards the dark mysteries of the Victorian drive.

22

This is a design that is evenly balanced between *form* and *content* of all kinds. Unity in such a restricted area is essential; basically this has been achieved by planning garden and living-room as one.

6A The paving of the terrace is carried inside the living room for a few feet. Note the mathematical relationship of the component parts.

6B A secondary paved area round an existing horse-chestnut is linked to the main terrace by a wide paved path. A cloistered effect connecting the two terraces was given by erecting horizontal beams on metal supports of the same dimensions as the living-room window frame.

6C A small pool with fountains runs across the end of the terrace. The line of it is carried on inside by a thick container for house plants.

The central space is covered with white gravel chippings which draw light down into the area and reflect artificial light from the house at night. It is easily cleaned.

Continued

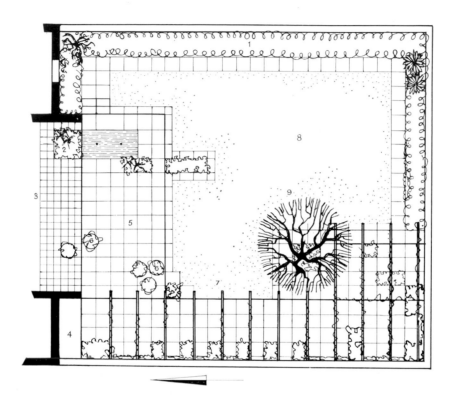

KEY TO PLAN

1. Shrubs
2. Indoor plants
3. Sitting room
4. Garden store
5. Raised terrace
6. Pots
7. Pergola
8. White gravel
9. Chestnut

24

6D Planting along the one sunny wall is the only complex feature.

25

Another small enclave which is chiefly a place to live in, but here living plants form the enclosures and divisions and the sky is a feature. The garden is surrounded by a high hornbeam hedge; inside, a planned disorder counteracts the frustrations of over-organised lives.

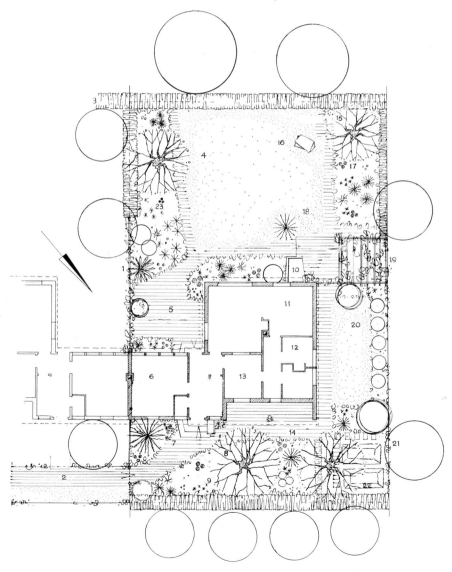

KEY TO PLAN

1. Trellis and climbing roses
2. Entrance
3. Hornbeam hedge
4. Sumach
5. Sitting space
6. Office
7. Yew
8. Cherry
9. Shade bed
10. Pool
11. Living room
12. Bedrooms
13. Kitchen
14. Plum
15. Field maple
16. Bird-bath
17. Flower beds
18. Rose New Dawn
19. Arbour
20. Soft fruit
21. Wooden fence
22. Compost
23. Polyanthus beds

7A The path to the house is on the north side, so the plants chosen are shade-tolerant. The tree is a *Prunus cerasus* (sour cherry)—white flowers for the owners in spring, dark red fruits for the birds in autumn.

27

7B The perception of nature here is so acute that even the blown leaves seem to acquire a meaning.

7C One of the two sitting areas (the other is in the shade). Large slabs of natural stone ensure a dry surface.

The Scottish climate and the site were the key factors here. To the north is a spectacular view; to the south a busy road that restricts privacy. The garden and the living part of the house are integral; one relies on the other in terms of visual enclosure, restriction of views and use of materials. The court is separated into a number of pockets, so that when the sun shines one can always find a corner that is free from wind.

8A The drop in level to the right of the house and the use of extended walls help to give an illusion of spaciousness as well as providing a series of viewpoints in the course of a walk round the outside of the house.

8B Water is secretly led in at the top of the free-standing wall and there is the pleasant sound of drops falling into the pool. A light under the water and floodlights onto the surrounding trees lend drama to the night view from the house.

The interlocking geometrical shapes of the house and its immediate surroundings are set in a simple, informal garden surrounded by trees. The interior of the house has been projected onto the half-enclosed terrace by the use of architectural forms.

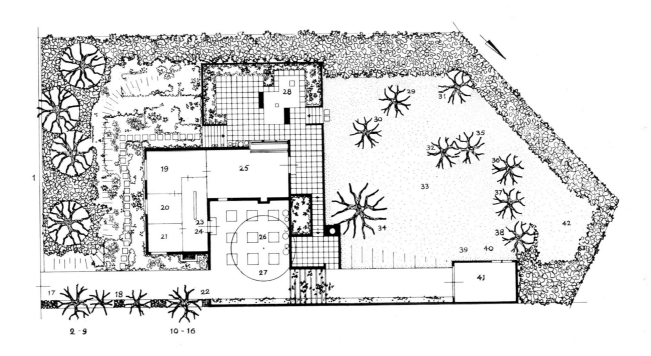

KEY TO PLAN

1. Road
2. Planting in front garden
3. Hedera Helix
4. Vinca minor
5. Corydalis lutea
6. Asperula odorata
7. Euonymus radicans
8. Cotula squalida
9. Anemone nemorosa
10. Gaultheria shallon
11. Rubus spectabilis
12. Cotoneaster adpressa
13. Telekis speciosa
14. Doronicum pardalianches 'Goldstrauss'
15. Heuchera hybrid 'Rakete'
16. Aconitum henryi
17. Sorbus aucuparia
18. Buddleia davidii
19. Dining room
20. Kitchen
21. Bedroom
22. Amorpha fruticosa
23. Hall
24. Hall
25. Living room
26. Gleditschia triacantha 'Inermis'
27. Decorative paving
28. Pool
29. Cornus kousa
30. Magnolia soulangeana
31. Euonymus europ.
32. Cornus florida
33. Lawn
34. Laburnum vossii
35. Halesia carolina
36. Crataegus submollis
37. Malus spectabilis
38. Morello
39. Prunus
40. Apricot
41. Garage
42. Compost

9A The steps leading up to the terrace court are reached by stepping-stones which wind through the informal front garden.

9B The terrace court.

9C The back of the house. The pergola that interrupts the long drive into the garage also stretches over the sheltered corner for sitting in the afternoon sun.

9D The reverse view of 9A, looking across the pool from the other side of the garden.

10 **HARMONDSWORTH,** Middlesex, England | John Brookes

The underlying abstract design that unites building and landscape is clearly apparent in this design. The landscape was worked off the building module, and on plan a Mondrian-type pattern emerged. Architects: John Spence and Partners.

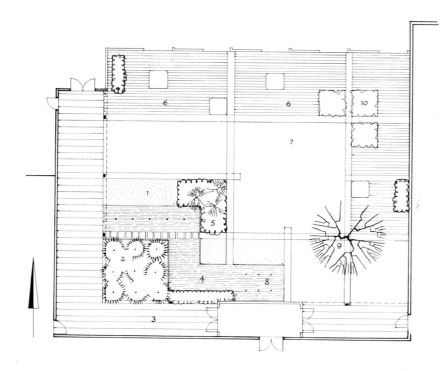

KEY TO PLAN
1. White chippings
2. Fastigiate trees
3. Covered way
4. Pool
5. Shrubs
6. Brick paving
7. Mown grass
8. Fountains
9. Specimen tree
10. Bedding

10A There is complete unity between house and garden. Note the concrete blocks with vertical shuttering which in fact provide occasional tables or benches, but which are an essential part of the abstract form.

10B The linear pattern was constructed in concrete slabs with infill panels of grass, water, planting or white gravel chippings.

10C A block of fastigiate robinias and bamboo gives solid vertical height.

10D In moist climates such as England's, the height of fountains must be variable according to the wind. In hot countries it is a pleasure to feel blown spray.

The garden of a model house in a seaside area. The site is terraced, with high banks at the back and an ocean view from the front of the house, which is 4–5 feet above street level.

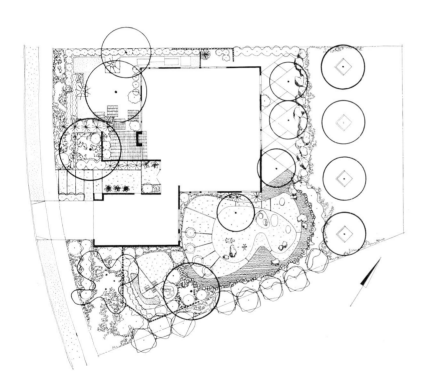

11A An ornamental play area for the children, outside the family room at the back. It can remain, with some redevelopment, when they no longer use it. The ground is surfaced with patterns of concrete and fir bark.

11B Yellow brick pads extend the terrace outside the living room. Here the adventure in abstract design is obvious and peculiarly successful.

11C A private patio for the parents.

38

Here is a garden in which the sculpture by Daphne Hardy-Henrion not only organises the design visually, but seems to summarise and express all that is meant by the words "poetic content". It is interesting to compare the figure with those on a Gothic cathedral, with which it has similarities of distortion. Gothic sculpture is elongated and distorted in harmony with its architectural surroundings; this figure appears distorted in harmony with the nearby tree forms.

12A The sculpture is in *ciment-fondu*. The raised flower-bed behind was formerly an enormous rubbish heap, too large to move. The continuous hard path round the garden (left foreground) has some exciting bends for tricycles and scooters.

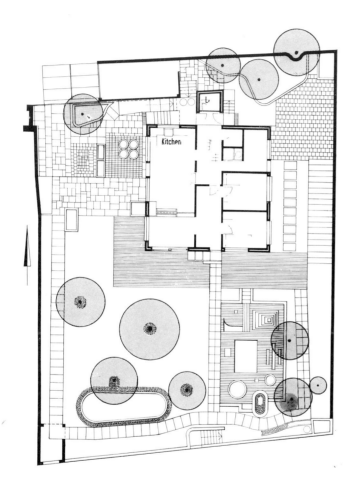

12B The sunk garden was already on the site. Its new three-dimensional abstract design will not be fully effective until the privet hedge matures.

12C The entrance court.

Kitchen

12D Mr. Manasseh designed the house
as well as the garden.

Two modern interpretations of the traditional Japanese garden. Both are interesting essays in the use of material, but it may well be that this technique is their main contribution to the study of modern garden design. Just as in western garden art we cannot rely upon the philosophy of history to motivate present-day design, so these gardens in external form may be less convincing in their relation to nature than, for instance, that in Plate 7B.

13B Okayama: Mr. Nakamura's garden. Here is a juxtaposition of stone forms that creates a relationship between observer and rock which is traditional to the east, and towards which the west is groping by trial and error.

13A Takamatsu: Mr. Usuki's garden. The timeless river of sand passes an ancient rock form. In all their gardens, whether historic or modern, the Japanese are prepared to give time to maintenance far surpassing the standards of the west.

Full advantage is taken of the sloping site : house and landscape are one, the landscape flowing through the house. To the east are magnificent views of the Surrey Hills. The west side looks across a courtyard of patterned grass and stones to the woods beyond. Apart from a few flowering shrubs, the garden is just grass and trees.

The owners, Mr. and Mrs. Calvert Carey, wanted not only a conversation piece and a setting for their contemporary sculpture, but also a place in which to relax and potter, a place in which to give parties. They did not want to wait years for the final effect, so trees weighing seven tons apiece came over the house by crane, temporarily re-routing Washington traffic.

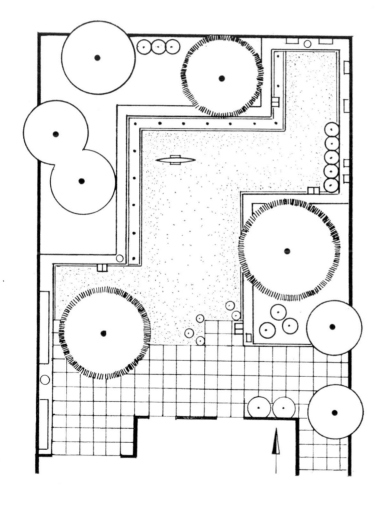

Surrounding the garden is a high brick wall; inside, in rectilinear pattern, is a low brick wall making places to sit or to put sculpture, and containing pockets for herbs and plants, white and blue clematis, English ivy and one "Peace" rose. Between the two walls are large rectangular planting beds with rose trees as well as flowers and ground cover. The floor of the garden is grass interrupted by sculpture, trees and narrow pools with fan-tailed fish and fountain jets.

15A Winter and summer, the three black pines *(Pinus Thunbergii)* dominate the garden. Their branches make picture frames for the sculpture. The dream of acquiring a cast of Henry Moore's "King and Queen" having faded, the outdoor collection began with two chimney-pots from an ancient English house in Surrey.

15B "Uranus II" by Hadju is walled in by a row of corkscrew willows *(Salix matsudana tortuosa)* and by many fountain jets. At night, the heavenly ancestry of this sculpture is fantastically obvious, for each of the twice seven columns of water is moon white and jittery. This is brought about by pinpoint lights concealed below water in the walls of the black slate pool.

15C "The Guitar Player" by Lipchitz guards that part of the garden which is like a woodland in miniature, with a path of pine needles. In the heavy shade of the Japanese black pine and the willows grow maidenhair and Christmas ferns, plantain lilies (hostas) and violets; in the light shade are blue common rues, phlox, liriope and Gumpo azaleas (varieties of *Rhododendron simsii eriocarpum).* All the planting was designed for easy maintenance.

Miss Colvin writes of her own garden: "The planting is intended to give continuous calm enjoyment at all seasons, rather than to dazzle the eye in the height of summer. The ground is well covered with low plants chosen for beauty of foliage: many are evergreen and there are masses of spring bulbs. In and over the ground cover plants are many flowering shrubs, roses, viburnums, hydrangeas, tree paeonies, etc., to provide flower all through the year.

"I have tried to get a feeling of quiet space in this small area, enclosed as it is by grey stone walls and farm buildings. I try, too, to engender a sense of anticipation and interest by the progression from one interesting plant group to the next in a rhythm, giving definite contrasts without loss of unity. But it is difficult to reconcile simplicity with one's enthusiasm for plants in so small a garden, and I probably let the plants jostle one another too much."

16A Fennel springs straight up from the ground, like fountain jets, but for the most part the plants are closely woven together so as to give each other support. For instance, *Gentiana septemfida* grows through tufts of low saxifrage. In the foreground: Bergenia, variegated deadnettle *(Lamium galeobdolen).* On the far side, rugosa roses behind plantain lilies (hostas), Solomon's seal and iris.

16B A bold group of giant hemlock *(Heracleum giganteum)* glimpsed between foliage. Under the chestnut tree, bulbs and a succession of low, shade-loving plants give interest all the year round—*Iris foetida*, aquilegias, campanulas, woodruff, varying cranesbills, cyclamen and autumn crocus. The leaves of the aquilegias and woodruff help to prop up the autumn crocus.

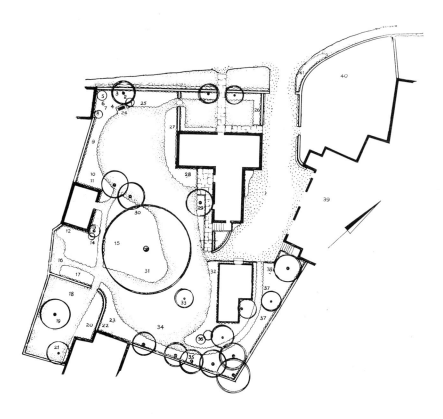

16C A curved sweep of contrasting foliage. In front, purple-leafed sage, red smoke plant *(Rhus cotinus purpurea)*, lilac spheres of *Allium albopilosum, Verbascum broussa* with downy silver leaves and lemon yellow flowers, iris and *Artemisia ludoviciana.* Behind, *Prunus eleagrifolia,* dusky *Rosa rubrifolia,* white delphiniums.

KEY TO PLAN

1. Rhus cotinus purpurea
2. Lilium regale
3. Pyrus eleagrifolia
4. Rosa rubrifolia
5. Prunus spinosa purpurea
6. Vitis purpurea
7. Clematis montana rubens
8. Rhus cotinus purpurea
9. Rugosa roses
10. Solomon's Seal
11. Lilies of the valley
12. Fig
13. Holly
14. Rosa Kiftsgate
15. Shade tolerant plants
16. Compost
17. Herbs
18. Bee yard
19. Liriodendron
20. Tree peonies and hellebore
21. Apple
22. Box
23. Heracleum giganteum
24. Seat
25. White delphiniums and
     grey foliage plants
26. Tree peonies and hardy cyclamen
27. Shrub roses
28. Lilium regale
29. Apple
30. Horse chestnut
31. Bulbs and low ground-cover
32. Low evergreens and lilies
33. Apple
34. Lawn
35. Scarlet willows
36. Viburnum tomentosum 'Lanarth'
37. Winter flowering plants
38. Rosa Iceberg and lilies
39. Garage
40. Fruit and vegetables
41. Acanthus spinosa

There is here a beautiful and complementary relationship between the extreme simplicity of the grass saucer, and the massed planting and carefully selected trees which it contains.

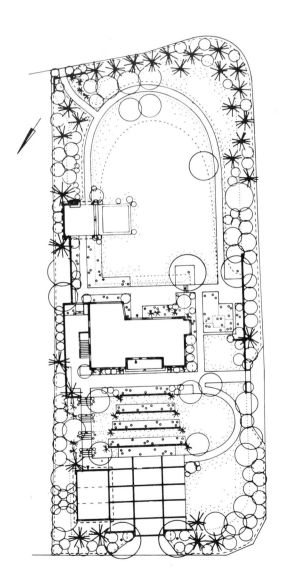

A garden on the slope of a Swiss mountain has as its only feature an arrangement of water, cut stone slabs, boulders and plants, which effectively links the sophisticated house with the rough landscape beyond. It is most interesting to compare the significance of the rock forms and their placing with those shown in Plate 13B. Here, the stones are lying down and are thus associated with the heavy stone paving.

Here is a very strong and well-proportioned architectural conception which relies upon the beautiful austerity of the machine-made walls acting as a foil to plant shapes.

18A Dining Recess

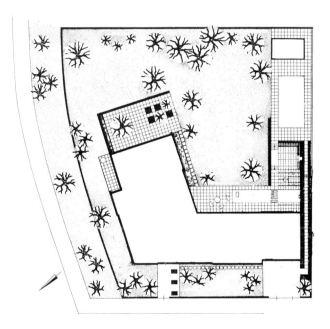

Opposite
18B Small trees break up the floor pattern of the bedroom court.

18D There is a sunbathing terrace beyond the sculpture, which emerges from the water of the pool.

18C The ornamental pool with aquatic plants such as small water lilies, Sweet Flag *(Acorus calamus variegatus), Pontederia cordata, Sagittaria lancifolia, Cyperus alternifolius.*

The Danish architect Arne Jacobsen has enclosed his own small terrace garden by thick hedges, within whose shelter grow the myriad plants which are to him a source of inspiration. The sense of geometry which informs the whole garden provides a discipline within which the plants can grow as exuberantly as they please. To preserve the view of the nearby Sound, there are no trees, but hedges and tall shrubs ensure that there is shade as well as sun.

KEY TO PLAN

1. Arundinaria murielae
2. Arundinaria nitida
3. Arundinaria auricoma
4. Sasa japonica
5. Sasa senanensis nebulosa
6. Taxus baccata
7. Larix leptolepsis
8. Miscellaneous perennials
9. Rodgersia podophylla
10. Hydrangea sargentiana
11. Pachysandra terminalis
12. Euonymus minima
13. Gunnera chiliensis
14. Orchids
15. Bird-bath
16. Miscanthus zebrinus
17. Miscanthus gracillimus
18. Avena sempervirens
19. Peonia arborea
20. Viburnum davidii
21. Rodgersia tabularis
22. Myrica
23. Paulownia tomentosa
24. Rhus typhina laciniata
25. Acer japonicum
26. Picea nidiformis
27. Hedera colchica
28. Asarum europeum
29. Berberis verruculosa
30. Rhus typhina
31. Stephanandra incisa
32. Metasequoia glyptostroboides
33. Stephanandra incisa
34. Cotoneaster salicifolia
35. Robinia pseudoacacia
36. Ulmus
37. Laburnum
38. Pyracantha
39. Cotoneaster dammeri
40. Hedera helix
41. Berberis polyantha
42. Crinum powellii
43. Peonia delavayi
44. Agapanthus
45. Hippophae
46. Eremurus robustus
47. Sorbus koemmeana
48. Yucca filamentosa
49. Pieris japonica
50. Erica carnea alba
51. Arundo donax
52. Pinus sylvestris
53. Ribes alpinum
54. Euphorbia lathyrus
55. Miscanthus variegatus
56. Veratum nigrum
57. Cotoneaster multiflora
58. Lilium henryi
59. Gypsophila repens
60. Gentiana asclepiadea
61. Gentiana sino ornata
62. Podophyllum emodi
63. Clematis macropetala
64. Hedera conglomerata
65. Prunus schipkaensis
66. Lilum gigantium
67. Hedera conglomerata
68. Fig tree
69. Clematis le coultre
70. Akebia quinata
71. Betula pendula
72. Dianthus
73. Taxodium distichum
74. Lonicera tragophylla
75. Pinus cembra
76. Berberis stenophylla
77. Prunus schipkaensis
78. Aristolochia durior
79. Lonicera henryi
80. Viburnum rhytidophyllum
81. Sitting place in sun
82. Sitting place in shade

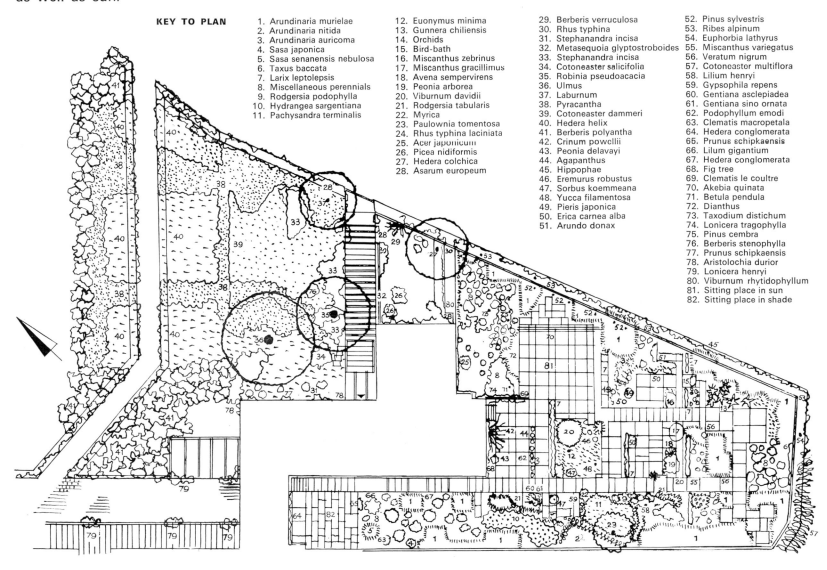

19A Yuccas rise from a sea of *Euonymus minima* and white winter-flowering heath *(Erica carnea alba)*. The huge leaves of a *Paulownia tomentosa*, linked by a *Hydrangea sargentiana* to the feathery fronds of bamboo *(Arundinaria murielae)* give privacy.

19B The view from the first floor. Architectural clipped hedges of varying heights create a series of small compartments.

19C Fritillaries and grape hyacinths against a clipped larch hedge. The larch, being deciduous and rather wiry, allows the air to circulate through the garden.

19D Plants are used like sculpture in this garden. A group of *Arundo donax.*

19E Looking back towards the house. The huge paving slabs are of grey limestone.

58

19F The delicate tracery of clematis and *Akebia quinata* against the walls of the sitting-place in the sun.

Five separate gardens united in one design surround Danish architect Eske Kristensen's house and office. The spaces are like additional rooms to the house, having as well their own particular furniture.

20A The outer wall is on a slope. It has been built in staggered, free-standing sections with planting in between—an original solution to a familiar problem.

20B Flagstones cross the pool and continue into the garden for the staff.

20C A table and benches of plain stone slabs.

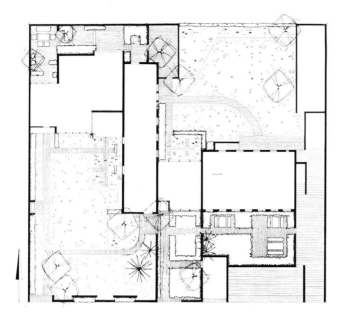

20D The entrance to the private garden.

20E The ornamental pool in the front garden, seen from the office.

20F The front garden and office entrance.

20G The reverse view of Plate 20E, from the office entrance.

The original site for this house and garden, with splendid native California live oaks, sloped towards a heavily-wooded ravine. Both the owner and the landscape architect wanted to establish a close relationship with the natural setting. She asked for a free-form swimming pool, thinking this would achieve it, but he felt that a circle (an elemental form found in nature) would rest more easily and with more assurance on the site. There is a harmony between geometrical and natural forms that is partly due to the masterly transition between circle and rocks; this is the very basis of landscape art.

21A The hillside between house level and pool is retained by large slabs of river-washed stone. As they step down to the pool, they create a waterfall, a small pool, and plant pockets for azaleas, a Japanese maple and other shade-loving colourful shrubs and flowers.

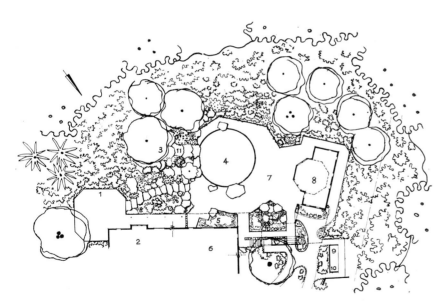

KEY TO PLAN

1. Wood deck	7. Brick terrace
2. Upper level	8. Pavilion
3. Waterfall	9. Filter
4. Pool	10. Storage
5. Deck	11. Waterfall
6. Lower level	

21B The pool coping and terrace are of textured buff-coloured brick, in contrast to the grey and brown stain of the redwood house and pavilion. The pool plaster is green, which gives it depth and a certain sylvan quality.

The garden nestles on a slope, with the house at the apex; the main entrance to the house is about sixteen feet above street level. The area is not big, but it appears to be huge because of the location of the house and the garden in the hilly, still empty landscape. The house has two wings at right-angles, giving wind protection to the sitting-place and extensive outdoor lobby.

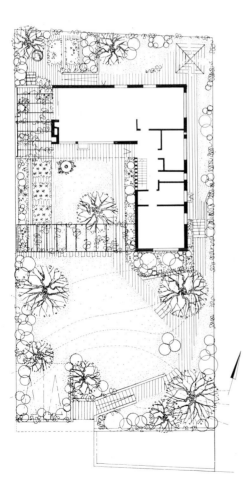

22A "Letting one's eyes wander about freely cannot be done indefinitely," says Mr. Schreiner. "A pergola forms a diaphanous frame serving as a foreground for a profound depth." From an old millstone a veil of water is sprayed out over the stone and surrounding cobbles, forever breaking and reflecting the light in new ways.

22B In spite of the considerable differences in height, there are but few walls in the garden. Instead, the ground was levelled off where necessary in soft curves and slopes which give a varied play of movement.

22C Tree, bush and flower, in addition to a little rose garden close to the house (left), provide the requisites of scale and colour that make up the garden, which is surrounded by vineyards and which has become a valued place for an elderly couple to live in and to find relaxation.

This garden lies in the villa quarter on the Zurichberg. The steeply-sloping terrain called for sharp terracing so as to make the best use of the ground, and the subtle use of levelling has resulted in an impression of great liveliness and variety. The climax is a strongly-modelled mound in the top corner. Plants are the predominant material used. The architect's wish to separate the house from the street has been realised by a dense plantation of hornbeam (*Carpinus betulus*) thickened with field maples (*Acer campestre*). The garden court and the living rooms are protected from observation by hazel (*Corylus avellana*), hawthorn (*Crataegus oxycantha*) and yew (*Taxus baccata*). Outside the living area is a large courtyard garden, the level of which is dropped outside the bedrooms, so as to give a slight air of remoteness. In the upper garden ramps make it easier to move garden equipment.

The big embankments in the lower garden are covered with small periwinkle (*Vinca minor*) and ivy (*Hedera helix*). Under the trees in the upper garden are shade-loving plants such as anemones (*A. nemorosa*), woodruff (*Asperula odorata*), wild strawberries (*Asarum europeum*), foxgloves (*Digitalis*), violets (*Viola odorata* and *silvatica*), veronica and wood sorrel (*Oxalis*). The beds near the house are filled with semi-shade loving plants—hellebores, astilbes and cranesbills.

23A The garden court and covered sitting place (1 and 9 on plan).

23B Stepping-stones lead past the end of the bedroom block and into the garden court.

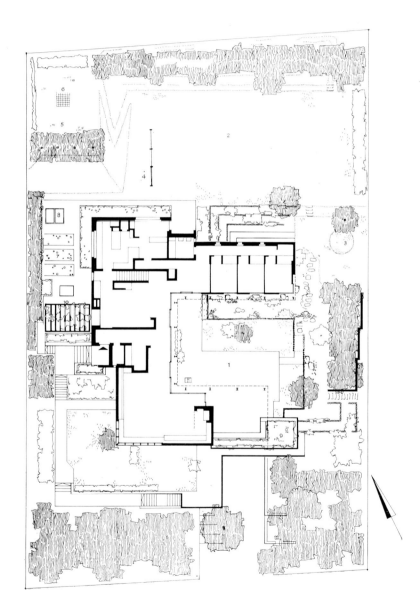

23C The grass lawn of the garden court is higher than the surrounding ground and is retained by thick timber posts which make an interesting contrast with the concrete walls of the flower-box at the end of the covered sitting-place.

KEY TO PLAN
1. Garden court
2. Playing field
3. Sand pit
4. Gymnastic apparatus
5. Mound
6. Fire
7. Flower garden
8. Forcing beds
9. Flower box
10. Pergola

23D The cutting garden.

The splendid view across a golf course has been kept as a surprise until the last possible moment. In order to catch this view, the house is raised up on walls which run out from the house to form terraces and outdoor rooms for large-scale entertaining. Architects: William Breger and Stanley Salzman.

24A The entrance. Walls and heavy planting conceal the view until the visitor enters the front door. The elm tree has been walled round at its existing level and surrounded by a raised evergreen garden of pachysandra, vinca and box enriched with bulbs and occasional foliage plants.

69

24B The walls of the living area are carried out on to the terrace, integrating house and garden.

KEY TO PLAN
1. Terrace
2. Living room
3. Dining room
4. Guest study
5. Bedroom garden
6. Bedroom
7. Parking forecourt
8. Entrance garden
9. Screened porch
10. Yard
11. Laundry
12. Maid
13. Garage
14. Service
15. Service court

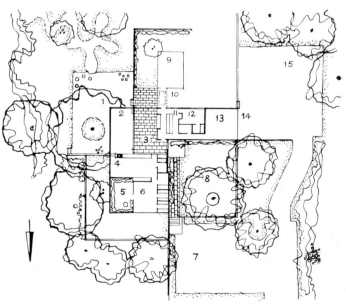

24C The swirling paths not only appear natural to their position (they could easily have been a "gimmick"), but in their sense of movement and direction link with the golf course beyond. Their colour ties up with the sand of the bunkers, strengthening the illusion that the fairway and greens are part of the estate.

A riverside strip between an old walled garden and the river Thames near Lechlade. The plants chosen were such as would help to effect the transition from garden to meadowland.

KEY TO PLAN
1. Cornus alba sibirica variegata
2. Gunnera manicata
3. River Thames
4. Salix vitellina
   chrysostella (pollarded)
5. Heracleum mantegazzianum
6. Rhus typhina
7. Hydrangea quercifolia
8. Shrubs and bulbs
9. Viburnum rhytidophyllum
10. Rough grass
11. Mown grass
12. Gunnera manicata
13. Populus alba

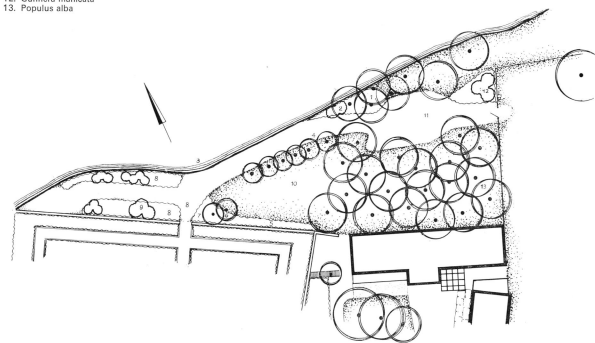

25B Grouped among white poplars and pollarded scarlet willows, *Gunnera manicata* and *Cornus alba variegata* provide contrasts of texture and colour.

House and garden are on a lake five miles long and one mile wide, whose shores are still rich in beautiful stretches of reeds—*Phragmites communis* and *Scirpus lacustris,* fine trees and unspoiled water-meadows.

The owner at first wished to have an imposing garden filled with flowers, roses and expensive shrubs. After much discussion, he finally allowed himself to be persuaded that, on such a site, the dominant requirement was to enhance and protect nature. The house and swimming pool are set away from the lake so as to be above flood level. Architects: Erwin P. Nigg and Egon Dachtler.

26A A raised wooden duck-walk leads to the lake.

26B The terrace.

"The house and its surroundings are lightly set in the meadow landscape."

26C The swimming pool.

26D The terrace, with the swimming pool in the background. Informal groups of shrubs link the garden with the natural landscape.

The forms and materials used in this garden are a sophisticated extension of the Mediterranean vernacular in the house itself. Hospitality plays a big part; the entrance to the front door is over broad concrete pads designed to give a feeling of generous welcome, and there is ample parking room for visiting cars. Architect: John Nordbak.

27A The swimming-pool terrace.
The fence is of redwood.

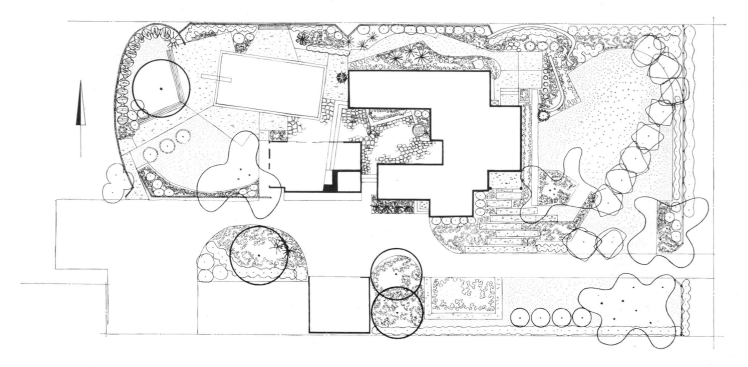

27B Across the north side of the house, formerly a dead space with few windows, a shade garden has been developed with overhead shelter. This makes it a pleasure to walk round the house.

27C A small patio outside the living-room is enclosed by the curving arms of two sculptured stucco walls.

28 **LACHEN,** Switzerland | Ernst Baumann

The strength and sense of permanence of rock and timber have inspired the design of this house and garden. The planting is restrained and complementary to this idea. In the garden, dark brown wood and uncut stone are seen against the smooth concrete walls of the house; this includes the architect's office, with its own small, secluded flower garden. The larger private garden is surrounded on three sides by trees—existing woodland and a row of hornbeams—and a wall. The south side is open to the view, with the boundary marked only by a row of rocks that also serve as seats.

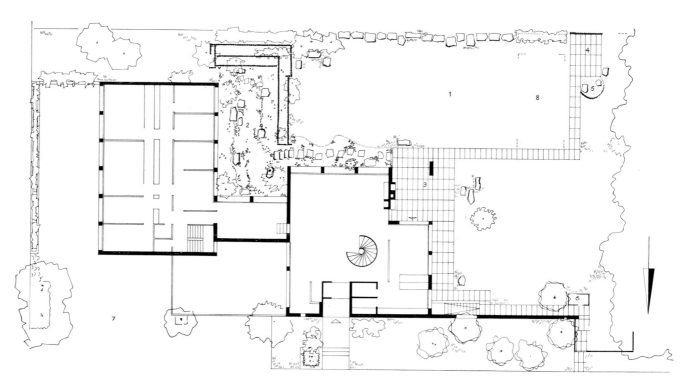

KEY TO PLAN

1. Private house
2. Flower garden
3. Covered sitting place
4. Sitting place at edge of the wood
5. Sand pit
6. Compost
7. Forecourt
8. Proposed swimming pool

28A Stepping stones lead past the windows of the house, towards the office garden.

28C The office garden. Wooden posts form the retaining walls and the palisade which prevents the office windows from overlooking the private garden.

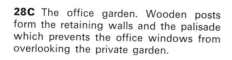

84

28D A small sandpit and groups of natural stones provide the accents in this simple, open garden.

28E From the windows of the house the view sweeps across the low rock wall, whose forms are associated with the distant view.

29 **WEXHAM SPRINGS,** Buckinghamshire, England | G. A. Jellicoe

Into an early nineteenth-century park landscape a new domestic garden for the Cement and Concrete Association's research station has been fitted. It was intended as an essay in the textures of artificial stone in relation to plants, but it is also an essay in the pure abstract design of contemporary painting.

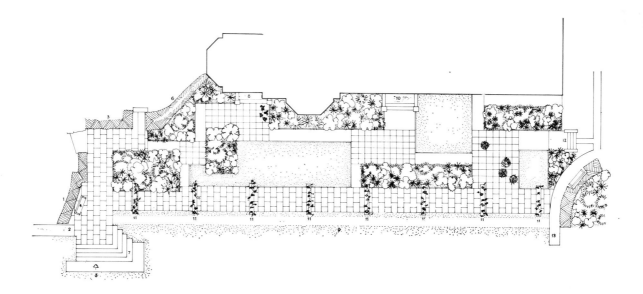

KEY TO PLAN

1. New yew hedge
2. Existing path
3. Existing yew
4. Seat
5. Up
6. Existing yew hedge
7. New concrete steps
8. Existing steps
9. Existing grass bank
10. Existing steps
11. Arches formed by trailing plants over light rod frames
12. Existing steps
13. Existing concrete path

29A The garden occupies a terrace between the house and a wide lawn leading to an open landscape. It is dominated at one end by the giant concrete fantasy by William Mitchell, cast *in situ*. The rich planting in the raised beds complements the flat pattern of grass and paving.

29B The green arches give a sense of rhythm and a feeling of enclosure; they are covered with vines and evergreen honeysuckle *(Lonicera japonica halliana)* —the vines for their quick growth and the honeysuckle for winter effect. In the foreground, the retaining walls of the raised bed are of blue-green concrete with a coarse black aggregate, designed to set off the grey foliage of lavender, sage and other scented plants which tumble over the sides.

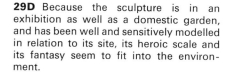

29C Nineteenth century and twentieth century in close embrace. Few arts other than landscape could comprehend and unify in a single view such differences in the ideas of time as well as space.

29D Because the sculpture is in an exhibition as well as a domestic garden, and has been well and sensitively modelled in relation to its site, its heroic scale and its fantasy seem to fit into the environment.

A design based on a fresh interpretation of traditional ideas, with eighteenth-century England as the source. The old Sussex house appeared to be sinking into the ground and was smothered in vegetation when it was bought by its present owners, Sir Walter and Lady Worboys, a few years ago. Since then, the ground at the back has been lowered to the level of the house and extended to make an informal platform, ending in a ha-ha; the line of a hedge has been lowered and the crowns of several oak trees raised. The result is a magnificent series of views over the Sussex Weald, in which the house is linked with the far landscape by receding clumps of trees, as in a painting by Claude Lorrain.

30A Outside the new wing of the house, a warm corner for sitting out is protected by shrubs and trees.

30B The entrance courtyard at road level, with steps down to the old level of the house. The alighting area is defined by stone setts. All the materials are traditional, but the shapes are original.

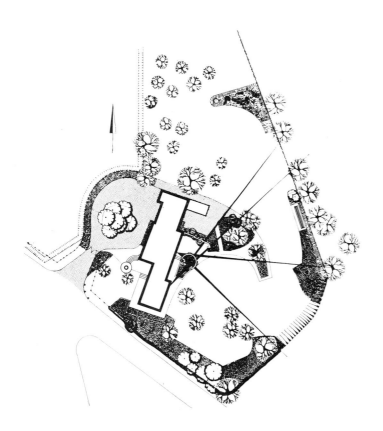

30C From the terrace outside the dining-room a crescent of paving and planting stretches out towards the view. Its curve brings the eye back again after contemplating the scene, making a unity of house and landscape. The viewing lines are shown on the plan.

The house is on a main road and is raised two feet above the garden level. The landscape architect's tasks therefore were to give a sense of spaciousness without sacrificing privacy, and to associate the elegant house with the garden.

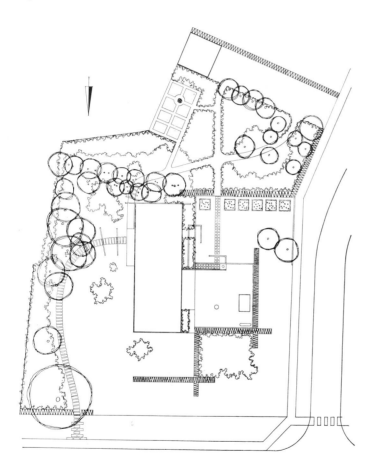

31A A path of precast concrete slabs winds from the road to the house door. To give the garden more depth on this side, there is no wall or hedge at the boundary line; the lawn merges with the grass which flanks the sidewalk, except for a brief low hedge where the path meets the road. Hornbeam hedges and shrubs give seclusion in the house and on the terrace.

31B On the west side, the problem of levels was solved by making a small paved flower terrace outside the sliding doors of the sitting-room. In contrast with the severe lines of the house, this terrace is splashed with patches of colour, like a big painter's palette. In one corner, a small pond with a fountain and a redwood seat provide another contrast, between straight lines and the natural forms of aquatic plants.

The abrupt contrast between wild woodland and the crystalline structure of the house has been carefully studied. The purpose is to give the inhabitants a vivid awareness of all the elements in nature. Architect: Ing. Böninger.

32A The garden side of the house. Dog-roses, foxgloves and raspberries flourish in the open; under the conifers are bilberries and moss cushions. A children's paradise.

32B The internal courtyard, for sun-bathing and games; planting is restricted to the minimum.

32C Since contrast with nature, not unity, is the aim, even the terrace is raised above the ground, so that the lines of the building remain absolutely clear.

The Villa Gadelius is on a steep slope on the northern shore of Kyrkviken bay. The architect, Ralph Erskine, felt the need to set off the hard, raw surfaces of his concrete architecture against a softer landscape background. This was done by means of turf-covered embankments. Now high and steep, now low and gently sloping, their rounded forms almost engulf the concrete walls or, as isolated hillocks, merge into the original landscape. On the roof of the villa is an enclosed garden with a place for sunbathing. This is a masterly and imaginative study in three-dimensional form.

33A Looking down on the bay from the roof. The mixed forest on the site has been thinned out to bring in light and air. Narrow vistas were cut through the trees at several points.

33C The roof garden, with the rounded domes of the villa's skylights. Plants which tolerate dry conditions were chosen: *Berberis Thunbergii, Potentilla fruticosa, Genista tinctoria, Rosa nitida, Festuca crinum ursi, Iris germanica, Achillea tomentosa, Erica carnea.* In the grass of the embankment on the right are wild flowers: *Galium verum, Achillea mille-folium, Campanula rotundifolia, Viola tricolor, etc.*

33B Ground modelling near the entrance.

33D Section.

Dr. Burle Marx is probably the only living landscape architect who is also an abstract painter; this quality informs all his work. The garden flows about and under the trees, around the rocks, in the shadow of the mango trees and spreads out into the pools of light of the clearings between the trees. The choice of a circular swimming pool has averted a break in the ebb and flow of the overall pattern. Architect: Dr. Henry Siso.

34A All the boulders and rocks were already on the site; it was only necessary to rearrange some of them. The mango trees were also preserved wherever possible and it is they which have determined the layout.

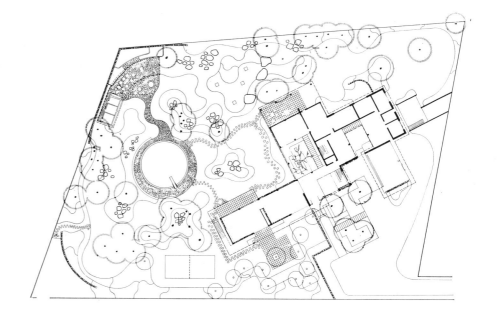

Plan: Many of the curves are simply divisions between different ground covers or grasses and plants. The curves have been used to give added interest in areas which have relatively low planting, and to make the eye follow the movement of the line in and out amongst the trees. In the tropics, plants left to their own devices soon become a small jungle, so a thin concrete barrier just below the surface of the soil is needed to keep the roots apart.

34B The high boundary walls had to be hidden from view in order to create a continuity with the backdrop of the mountains. Here, the vista is closed by a pavilion to house the changing rooms.

34C The internal garden. The pool from which the plants emerge, aided by sprinklers hidden in the top of the tree, creates the humid conditions that these plants enjoy in their natural habitat.

34D The internal garden, seen from outside.

This is clearly a garden primarily for hospitality rather than domestic use. It is a series of enclosures, in which people move from one dramatic viewpoint to another. At one moment you are cut off from the outside by a wall, the next instant you can see over the top, and finally you look through it where an opening has been made. The garden is built into a hillside, so that the sophisticated concrete enclosures, the wild meadow grass and the tree-fringed slopes form a complete cycle of contrasts.

Left:

35A The trees on the island are olives. Behind, the concrete wall backs on to a solid phalanx of eucalyptus trunks.

Right:

35B The splash of the fountain is the third element in the trio of sight, scent and sound.

In a broad, domestic landscape, house, garden and scenery are united by a harmonious sense of scale. For the sake of a wider view over the River Elbe, the house is set at the top of a slight rise and is raised upon a platform several feet high, with a brick retaining wall. It is surrounded by grass and trees except on the south side, where a formal garden has been made.

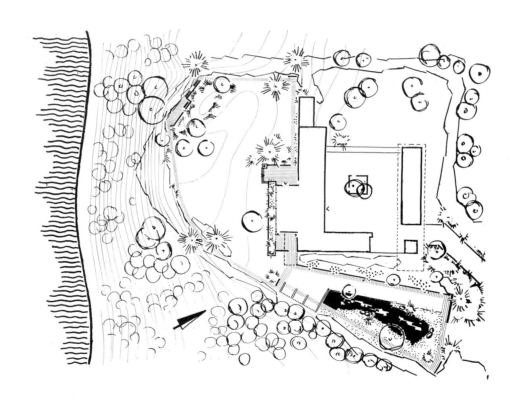

36A The view to the river. In the foreground, the top of the brick retaining wall on the river side of the house is treated as a giant window-box.

36B The high white brick wall that cuts across the end of the grass walk, and acts as a counterpoise to the pergola, is itself in the nature of an abstract.

36C The backbone of the formal garden is the broad grass walk. A brick wall nine inches high separates the grass from the shrubs in front of the house. On the left of the path is a large pool which is enclosed by a stone coping at one end but ends informally at the other.

The owners of the Villa Lefebure and their landscape architect were united in wishing to keep the many pines and ilex which were already on the site. It became, therefore, a question of small touches, of moulding the trees, the house and the new swimming pool into a pleasing whole, without disturbing the *genius loci* that the pines in their serried lines had already created.

An old ilex alley leads to the house, which lies slap across the rectangular site—a bulwark against the world outside. Beyond the pine wood the ground drops sharply into a hollow; here the swimming pool was constructed, out of sight from the house. Architects: Monaco and Luccichenti.

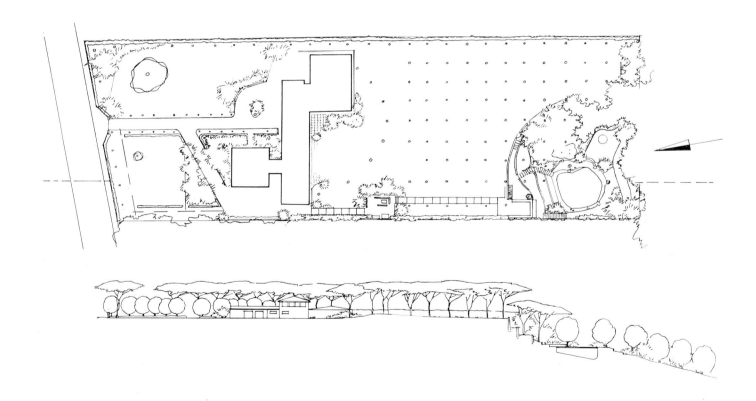

37A The pool, set in a remnant of what was once the vegetation of all the hills north of Rome—oaks *(Quercus pubescens)*, elms *(Ulmus communis)* and hazel *(Corylus avellana)*. The pool has sunshine almost all day, but the water is slightly heated, because the natural water is very cold.

37B Under the pines *(Pinus pinea)* the ground undulates slightly. Because water cannot penetrate the heavy clay soil, but runs over the surface, even the gentlest slope had to be carefully shaped and drained.

37C The south, garden side of the house, seen from beside the barbecue with its shady canopy of acacias. Beyond the sun-terrace, planting screens the grandparents' flat.

37D Retaining walls were necessary on the steep slope leading from the pine wood to the pool. They are of pink tufa and a rosy coloured stone called St. Elia, This pink and the varying greens of the pines and ilex and certain maquis-type shrubs are the only colours in the garden, except for a few clumps of iris, valerian and gazanias growing in the cracks in walls and paving.

A garden that is being made for pleasure, over the years, by its architect owner. Although on the boundary of Harlow New Town, it is remote and surrounded by agricultural land.

The architect's particular interest in garden design is the formation of spaces, by means of land shape and plants, which have diversity between them and which together make one total design of marked individuality. Here, the spaces range from those surrounding the house which, having an architectural association, are subject to a geometric discipline—flat planes and the right-angle—to those most remote in the valley, where the environment is completely natural. These two extremes in spatial character and those between them are unified in the first place by supra-spaces, that is, large spaces which embrace smaller ones by means of vistas and distant prospects; secondly, they are unified by limiting the range of plant material. Finally, the garden is made a complete whole by the personality of the designer; it is in his handwriting, so to speak.

38A From the sitting-room. As grass is a favourite plant of the designer, lawns surround the terraces and fall away into paddocks and then descend to the water meadows in two broad sweeps.

38B A splendid avenue of old limes leads from the house down to the wood, where Mary Gorrara's "Swan" stands in a small clearing. The wild area is a series of gardens each with a distinctive character, through which paths and steps are so threaded that the views are restricted and the spectator is led from one ambience to another.

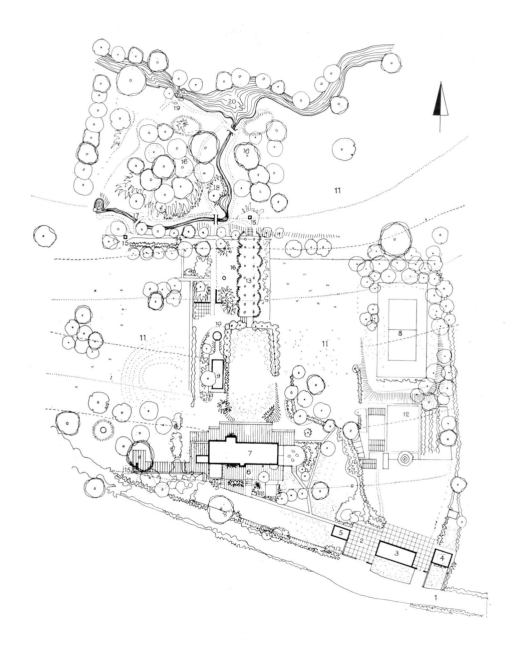

KEY TO PLAN

1. Marsh lane
2. Forecourt
3. Stables
4. Cottage
5. Garage
6. Terrace
7. The house
8. Tennis court
9. Pool
10. Gazebo
11. Paddock
12. Vegetable garden
13. Lime walk
14. Hazel walk
15. Sculpture
16. Wild garden
17. Stream
18. Bog garden
19. Waterfall
20. Pool

38C One of the series of enclosed wall gardens on the south side, seen from the sitting-room.

38D Another of the enclosed spaces, this time a breakfast court outside the main bedroom.

38E The brook, which is wide and deep enough for boating, was dammed to make a pleasant waterfall and to keep the water level constant; it was bulldozed out at its junction with the stream to form a pool.

38F A spring and tiny stream flowing into the brook were used as a basis for a water and bog garden where bamboos, ferns, hostas and other moisture-loving plants thrive.

38G Another small enclosed space by the house.

The most striking feature of this French Riviera garden is the tremendous scale of the drift-planting. It is this that relates the garden to the majestic landscape in which it is set.

The garden is a large one and is designed to be seen by its owner, M. Boussac, for only six weeks in the spring.

39A In the foreground are drifts of *Dimorphotheca Arctic Star* and *Cineraria maritima.* Under the Aleppo pines is a *maquis* of *Agathaea coelestis,* mesembryanthemums, rosemary, coronilla and medicago, used in swathes of two to three hundred each.

39C A drift of *Iris stylosa*, about sixty feet long and twenty feet wide, through which one ascends for about fifteen paces, giving a sense of leisure and ease.

39B *Cineraria maritima* under the pines.

39D Part of an earlier garden, rocky and steep, was dug up, and hundreds of aloes were added to those already there. Extra colour is introduced by mimosas, of which there are several different varieties *(Acacia cyanophylla, cultriformis, Claire de Lune,* etc.). In the sunny areas sheets of lavender alternate with masses of mixed zonal pelargoniums, which grow rampantly in the region, looking very different from the tidy bedding out of a municipal park.

39E The rocks and water belong to an earlier garden of 1900, but the broad drifts of underplanting are modern. It has been the intention to retain here a period atmosphere, by using Princess of Wales violets, tiny freesias, double stocks and pansies. *Jasminum polyanthum* (red buds, white flowers) climbs over trees and rocks, sending out waves of strong scent.

There is something of the free English garden and of the formal Italian garden in the composition and distribution of space here, but the meticulously-designed details have an affinity with modern abstract art.

From an artificial depression at one end of the park the ground rises gradually, terminating in an embankment planted with shrubs and trees that creates a green skyline. The surrounding landscape, flat and dreary, becomes invisible from within.

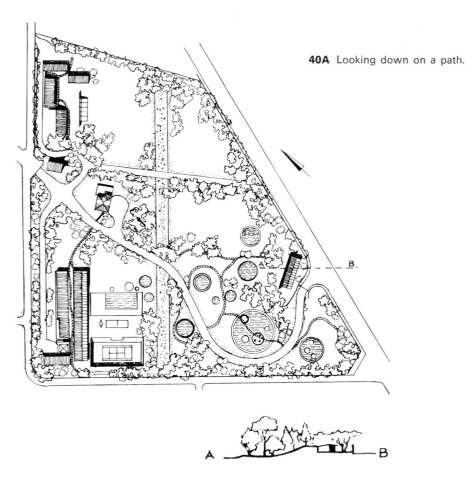

40A Looking down on a path.

40B The guests' pavilion looks across a
broad lawn.

40C An abstract composition in the paving round the swimming pool.

40D All the year round, flowers massed on either side of the main avenue provide the only bright colour. Otherwise, this is a green garden. The artificial green skyline can be seen on the further side of the avenue, which cuts across the middle of the picture.

Some of Sir Robert Sainsbury's collection of modern sculpture has spilled out into the garden. For the most part it is set under trees, amongst the green of hellebores, hostas and epimediums, or beside the yews under which sheets of cyclamen grow.

Opposite
41A The heroic scale and aloofness of the Henry Moore sculpture is superbly set in its plain green environment. The grass lawn rises gently to conceal a ha-ha, so that there is no visual break between the garden and the rolling Berkshire land-scape.

42 **KIPPEN,** Stirlingshire, Scotland | William Gillespie

Set in a hollow below a natural viewing terrace, the circular pool is the culminating feature of a large garden. Together with the adjoining straight line of the canal, it is particularly meaningful as a piece of organised geometry in an unorganised world. It successfully effects the transition from the domesticity of the garden to the wild landscape of the Forth basin and the Ochill hills—one of the most difficult tasks in the whole field of landscape design.

Opposite
The viewing terrace is reached by ninety-four steps of split larch risers and gravel treads, some of which can be seen in the centre foreground. The pool has a 30 foot fountain jet which can bring two new elements to the scene—movement and sound. When the waters are still they reflect the bridge and an enormous conifer.

ACKNOWLEDGEMENTS

We are greatly indebted to the landscape architects and other designers whose work is shown here, for their generosity in sending drawings and photographs. We should also like to thank those who sent material which we were reluctantly unable, for various reasons, to include. Acknowledgement is also made to the following photographers:

Architectural Press, 8a

Morley Bauer, 21a, 21b and 35b

Walter Bauer, 33a, b and c

Ernst Baumann, 23a, b, c, d and 28a, b, c, d and e

W. C. J. Boer, 9a, b, c, d and 18a, b, c, d

John Brookes, 5a, b, c; 6a, b, c, d; 10a, b, c; 30b and c

Andreas Bruun, 4

Cement and Concrete Association, 2a, b and c

Ronald A. Chapman, 3a and b

Lester Collins, 15a, b and c

Croydon Advertiser, 14b

John Dewar Studios, 8b

Roy Flamm, 35a

Alexandre Georges, 24a, b and c

J. St. B. Gruffydd, 30a

Ideal Home, 14a

Arne Jacobsen, 19a, b, c, d, e and f

Susan Jellicoe, 12b, c, d; 16a, b, c; 25a, b; 29a, b, c, d; 38a, c and d

Eywin Langkilde, 20a, b, c, d, e, f and g

Walter and Klaus Leder, 17a and b

Leonard Manasseh, 12a

F. Maurer, 26a, b, c and d

Moerheim, 31a and b

Sidney Newbery, 41

Sigrid Neubert, 32a, b and c

Russell Page, 39a, b, c and d

Studio Picca, 37a, b, c and d

Pietro Porcinai, 1a, b, c and 40a, b, c, d

Otto Rheinlander, 36a, b and c

Richard Schreiner, 7a, b, c and 22a, b, c

Evans L. Slater, 11a, b and c

Henk Snoek, 38b, e, f and g

John Stoddart and Fernando Tabora, 34a, b, c and d

Frank J. Thomas, 27a, b and c

Printed in Great Britain by
Willmer Brothers Limited, Birkenhead